A SHORT GUIDE TO
BREXIT
OUR DIVIDED
FUTURE

Atta Ul Haq

authorHOUSE®

AuthorHouse™ UK
1663 Liberty Drive
Bloomington, IN 47403 USA
www.authorhouse.co.uk
Phone: 0800.197.4150

Published by AuthorHouse 08/24/2016

ISBN: 978-1-5246-6166-3 (sc)
ISBN: 978-1-5246-6180-9 (hc)
ISBN: 978-1-5246-6165-6 (e)

1

INTRODUCTION

'Waiting hurts. Forgetting hurts. But not knowing which decision to take can sometimes be the most painful' (Jose N. Harris).

Britain votes to leave the European Union.

On Friday 24rd June 2016, as many bleary eyed people woke up to start their morning, and people like me checked the results of the vote on social media and mobile apps, they realised that their country had changed forever. 17,410,742 people voted to leave, 51.9% of the electorate, whilst 16,141,241 voted to remain, representing 48.1% of the vote. Unlike general elections where the turnout is relatively low, 72.2% of the UK's population voted on an issue which was to change the way their economy, democracy and political system would function. For some people this referendum resembled a vote to regain sovereignty and a chance to control immigration, whilst others saw it as a decision that could harm Britain's economic standing in the world.

To call this result the 'people's revolt' or a 'political earthquake' would certainly not be an overstatement. Speaking to many people across the UK, I came across many individuals who had never voted in their whole life, but came out for the EU referendum because they felt it was something they had to be part of. Irrespective of whether the campaign was fought fairly, one thing is clear: voters were energised within the political debate on a level which has never been seen before. Also, regardless of it being a negative or positive result, this vote represented a deep resentment many people had with the metropolitan elite, who at times ignored their concerns about the free movement of people and the EU's ever increasing role in British politics. From small British shires, to Labour's Northern heartlands, ordinary people voiced their opinion about a political project which they felt had not worked in their interest.

The problem with the post-Brexit analysis, and even with the referendum campaign on both sides, was the insistence on inundating the electorate with countless facts, figures and expert opinions. X number of businesses will leave their headquarters in London if we vote to leave, or X number of migrants from Turkey or Albania will come to the UK if they join the EU. On many occasions, a deluge of numbers often confuses rather than enlightens. In all this midst of press conferences, expert interviews and political soundbites, the voice and concerns of the ordinary man or woman was simply not heard in enough detail. Experts are important, and it would be harsh to completely dismiss their judgement, however the voices of ordinary citizens must also be projected on an equal level. Our insistence on listening to the experts and the elite, has meant that ordinary people are now expressing their political opinions on other forums and online platforms such as Facebook, Twitter and even Snapchat. I even witnessed this myself as I trawled through different social networks after the referendum result, where I saw how a plethora of online arguments and discussions had been initiated alongside online petitions, calling for a second referendum or for certain parts of the country to be made independent following the leave vote.

This book is a layman's guide to the referendum result, analysing and discussing the numerous factors which led to a vote to leave the European Union. It focuses on Britain's uncertain future outside the EU, looking at the issues the country will face and also the opportunities which await the country after it looks towards the ever-changing world. Exclusive comments by leading political figures, both from the leave and remain side, have been featured, where they express how they see Britain's economic and political future in the long term. I hope that this book serves as a blueprint for a post Brexit Britain, once which is optimistic, outward-looking and prosperous.

2

A QUARRELLING MARRIAGE

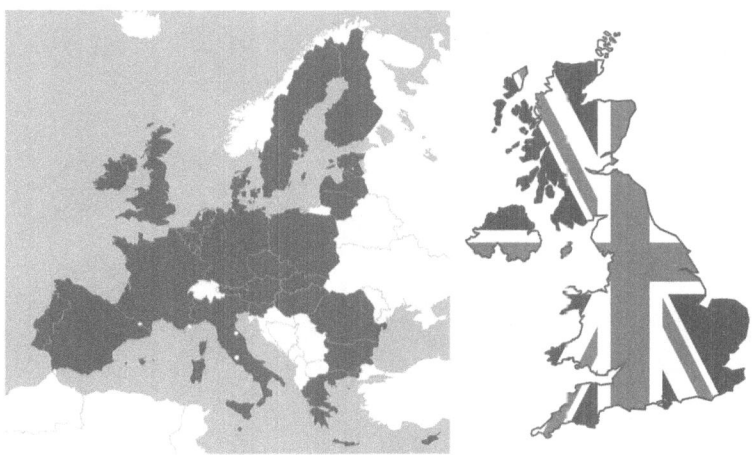

The EU was formed to bring Europe's nations more closely together so that they could never cause damage or hurt each other ever again. However, Britain's relationship with the EU could be described as a marriage which never seemed to work. Full of quarrels, arguments, bold statements and personality clashes. The fact is that Britain often asked too much from the European Union and the political bloc could not afford to give any such major concessions, in fear that other member states could follow suit. I will try to explain the UK's complicated relationship with the EU through a brief overview of events.

UK- EU relations have always been complicated and fractious

Under Prime Minister Edward Heath, Britain was finally allowed to become a member of the European Economic Community (EEC) in 1973. Britain's continued membership was put to a referendum in 1975, in which 67% voted in favour of membership – only the Western Isles and Shetlands voted 'No'. The tables have certainly changed now. The most striking thing about the 1975 referendum was that opposition strongly came from the left of the Labour party, from figures such as Michael Foot and notably Tony Benn. This opposition possibly represented the opening cracks between Britain and the political project.

Britain's major economic shock with the EU occurred on 16 September 1992, dubbed as Black Wednesday, when Britain was forced to withdraw the pound from the Exchange Rate Mechanism (ERM) under a Conservative led government. The ERM was an economic system which aimed to reduce the variability in exchange rates and Britain was unable to keep the pound above its lower limit which was agreed. Shortly after this economic shockwave, UK-EU relations hit another low when John Major faced a major backbench rebellion in his party over the Maastricht Treaty in 1993, a divide which has carried on in the 21st century with the prominence of Euroscepticism in the Conservative Party.

Interestingly enough, British politicians have often had a habit of bold statements and political adventurism against the European Union which has primarily been done to appease their respective parties. In a 1988 speech in Bruges, Margaret Thatcher strongly rejected a European super-state which she thought was exerting more dominance in domestic and national politics. This speech was particularly important as it resembled a shift towards a direct confrontation between the UK and EU, something which has characterised modern politics. Again, in September 2011, as EU leaders were trying to solve their problems through implementing a new treaty which set new budget rules, David Cameron vetoed the treaty becoming the first British Prime Minister to ever do so. Often acts like these would be a method of shoring up support amongst right-wing Eurosceptic MPs who did not see the EU as vehicle that could bring Britain prosperity. In this respect, the offering of the referendum by the Conservative government represents this, as David Cameron's Eurosceptic backbench MPs would find any opportunity to hold the governments feet to the fire over Europe.

During the referendum campaign, David Cameron assured the British public that he would renegotiate Britain's terms of membership inside the EU, one which would be in the best interest of the country. Things soon turned sour. Touring most of Europe in a whirlwind tour of talks, meetings and discussions, he soon found out that the European Union was not willing to accommodate the UK to a large extent. Cameron did not achieve all that he wanted, and there was no substantial treaty change. As we all know, things after that went downhill between the EU and Britain.

This quarrelling marriage was simply based on two entities who never seemed to listen to each other. Britain constantly rejected the notion of an 'ever closer union' and the EU did not like this. What the EU must learn from this relationship is that it needs to be more flexible with other member states. Simply refusing to listen to member state concerns puts the EU's future under risk, as the desire for more freedom and autonomy is increasing within many European countries. Directives that are drafted in by the EU must accommodate for the needs of individual member states who may or may not agree with certain proposals.

3

WHY DID WE VOTE TO LEAVE?

Although there are numerous factors which explain why Britain voted to leave the EU, some are more important than others. Concerns over freedom of movement, the rise of UKIP and increasing EU involvement in British politics, produced a cocktail of grievances which pushed the leave campaign forward. The reasons why people voted to leave the European Union must not be dismissed, but need to be analysed in more detail to understand the deep disconnect voters have with politics. Looking at these reasons in more depth will help policy makers and future governments to address some of the underlying causes which have led to a more divided Britain. If our political class fails to recognise the reasons for Brexit, they risk alienating further sections of our population, leading to uprisings which might be hard to control.

The rise of UKIP

UKIP had always been seen as a protest party, apparently one for 'fruitcakes, loonies and closet racists' as David Cameron once famously said in 2006. Traditionally, the party performed well in the European Parliamentary elections due to its Eurosceptic stance, where it came 2nd, behind the Tories in the 2009 European Parliament elections. 2014, however, was a turning point. Campaigning heavily upon the detrimental impact of EU free movement on public services and wages through its bold posters and campaign tactics, UKIP came first in the 2014 European Parliament elections where it sent the highest contingent of British MEPs to Brussels and gained 26.60% of the vote share.

The striking thing about UKIP is its fluid nature of politics. Neither does it represent the Left or the Right which is conventionally concerned with debates regarding market or state interference and low taxation versus high taxation. UKIP's message merges its stance on the EU with ideas surrounding nationalism, social conservativism and patriotism. This sort of message resonates with many voters, particularly in the North who have felt that globalisation has forgotten them. The real political earthquake occurred in the 2015 General Election, when UKIP gained 12.6% of the vote share with 3.8 million votes, however it only gained one MP. Attracting Tory voters in the South, and disaffected Northerners in the Labour heartlands, UKIP used the anti-EU sentiment to its full advantage. Where mainstream parties failed to address concerns over the free movement of people in fear of alienating certain voters, UKIP and its leader Nigel Farage crossed the barrier of political correctness and exploited the ways in which EU migration was supposedly having an impact in terms of lower wages, a breakdown in community cohesion and increased crime.

Being a party purely focused on the EU, UKIP, negatively or positively, engaged the electorate in regards to Europe. The politics of nationalism, national identity and community became even more prominent following UKIP's rise after 2012/2013, as issues of democratic deficit, uncontrolled migration and multiculturalism were brought to the forefront of the party. Although the EU was not responsible for all of the country's problems, UKIP painted it as such, giving many politically disconnected voters an entity to blame their woes on. The threat from the 'foreign' i.e. the EU, which UKIP often projected, struck many disillusioned, working class voters who had been disadvantaged through years of deindustrialisation. A clear example of this is the referendum result, where key places in Labour heartlands in the North, such as Sunderland, Doncaster and Hartlepool all voted to leave the European Union. In Hartlepool, for example, 69.6% of the electorate voted to leave. And these are the same areas in which UKIP came a very strong 2nd in the 2015 General Election.

UKIP, under Nigel Farage was energised into a proper political movement. The pint holding image of the leader reinforced the party's appeal amongst many sections of the electorate, who saw him as someone who they could relate to. It's hard to imagine another political party leader who is able to mingle and engage with ordinary people with such ease. Almost single-handedly, Nigel Farage brought together chunks of disaffected voters and brought them closer to the Brexit cause.

However, in my opinion UKIP has done more harm than good. Its central focus on immigration has often meant that it has exaggerated the negative implications of immigration to such a large extent that it has caused fractures in our society. As the EU issue gained traction during 2012/2013, UKIP's rhetoric starting painting migrants as a burden on society, without highlighting the positive contribution they made.

Freedom of movement within the EU

Immigration. Immigration. Immigration. If there was one word I could use to describe the main factor which led to a leave vote, it would certainly be immigration. Constant opinion polls during the referendum campaign, including many from the polling agency, Ipsos MORI, showed that voters rated the economy and immigration as the two most important issues that would determine how they voted. Freedom of movement within the EU is the cornerstone of the political bloc, which was established through the Treaty of Maastricht in 1992. Ever since that, it has remained a subject that has dominated British politics in one way or the other. It is not that people are necessarily against foreign people – but that the flow of people into certain communities is creating tensions and exacerbating existing issues.

The problem with immigration is that many of the leading political party leaders in British politics have consistently failed to address the concerns many people have with uncontrolled immigration from the EU member states. Immigration, for too long, was considered a taboo subject, felt to be too politically incorrect to mention in public discourse. What many Westminister politicians have failed to recognise is that uncontrolled immigration from the EU has led to depressed wages for lower paid workers who are the most vulnerable. For example, the House of Lords Economic Committee reached the following conclusion in 2008:

> 'The available evidence suggests that immigration has had a small negative impact on the lowest paid workers in the UK and a small positive impact on the earnings of higher paid workers'.

Any person who speaks about free movement in any negative way, or criticises the way it is unsustainable or discriminatory against non-EU migrants, is generally labelled as a racist to be frank. In that case, the referendum result could be seen as a victory against an out-of-touch elite who sneered at decent, working class concerns. Even many on the political left, such as Labour MP's Kate Hoey, Gisela Stuart and Frank Field argued during the referendum campaign that uncontrolled migration presented new burdens in terms of housing, public services and social cohesion. Many people who voted to leave, did not do so in order to pull up the drawbridge, but in order to have a fair immigration system in which people with skills that the country needed could be welcomed. The slandering of people who dared to question anything to do with immigration, produced an overwhelming result for the leave campaign.

Immigration was also a defining factor of this referendum because the public simply had enough of broken promises. David Cameron, in his election manifesto promised to reduce migration to the UK to 'tens of thousands'. Statistic after statistic showed that this commitment was a farce because immigration cannot be controlled if you are a member of the European Union due to the free movement of people. Figures released by the Office for National Statistics in May 2016, a month before the referendum, showed that net migration to the UK rose to 333,000 in 2015 – this was the second highest figure on record. In terms of EU-only net migration, the figure was 184,000. Despite these huge figures, the remain campaign still insisted that it would be possible to control EU migration through other means such as the benefit restrictions which were part of David Cameron's EU renegotiation. It was also very clear that European Union leaders and officials were not willing to compromise on the free movement of people which further angered voters.

From speaking to many voters who voted to leave, it was obvious that they were frustrated about the freedom of movement. This wasn't just expressed by the white, working class voters usually shown in the media, but also by people from ethnic minority groups. Many people from BME backgrounds were upset over the discriminatory nature of EU migration. Many wanted to bring their family members to the UK from different Commonwealth countries, even for short visits but could not do so due to strict immigration guidelines, whereas freedom of movement within the EU was lax and open to everyone.

Regardless of whether immigration concerns were exaggerated or not, remains an ongoing question, however future governments and political leaders must learn to address voter concerns, even if issues are sometimes not politically correct. The free movement of people within the EU is not sustainable for a globalised world, and the EU will soon have to re-think this.

Disconnect with the EU

Sometimes Brussels feels quite far away.

As with political parties, voter disconnection with the EU had increased. Many people who I had spoken to in the run-up to writing this book, suggested that they did not really dislike the EU, but could not really connect to it as they did with other causes. I completely agree. The main problem is that whenever the European Union had enacted a positive law for British people, be it a directive on working conditions or a law in regards to environmental protection, our politicians and governmental institutions have not highlighted this to the British people. They have either been too lax or simply ignorant when it comes down to telling the public about the key role that the EU has often played in bringing together the nations of Europe together under a single vision. However, when things go wrong our institutions and public figures are very quick to point their fingers towards the EU in blame. I consider this imbalance between highlighting the positive and negatives as one of the major reasons why the British people voted to leave the bloc. People were made to feel as if the EU was the root cause of problems such as the migrant crisis or the financial situation in Greece, whilst the underlying causes were often not thought about.

This disconnect was also caused due to a lack of information about the EU. In the process of writing this book, I asked several people regarding their knowledge of the EU and its related institutions. Only a small number actually knew who their MEP was and an even smaller number knew the different roles the EU carried out. Such an information deficit was caused due to media and government underreporting of the what the EU has done as I mentioned earlier. Secondly, appetite for political engagement has declined over time in many Western countries. The EU simply represents another layer to the political bureaucracy which many people are not interested in.

The other disconnect was purely due to the EU's negligence. As it operates through a system of pooled sovereignty, the EU implements laws/directives on a European scale where there is often a 'one-size-fits-all' policy approach. Such an approach simply fails to recognise variations in individual member states would may or may not benefit from some proposed legislation. Britain is a patriotic nature and values its system of parliamentary sovereignty – the EU has been accused of conflicting with it on many occasions. The European Communities Act 1972 recognises the primacy of EU law over UK law which has created many 'difficulties' for Britain. Let me give a small example. The EU's fisheries policies impose quotas and fishing limits on British fishermen so that each member state has equal access to the waters and to prevent member states from gaining an advantage over each other. This has reduced the zone available exclusively for British fishermen to operate on and has meant that British fishermen have to share waters with other fishermen from different countries. This is one example – there are many others that I could include in this book. From law and order to agricultural policy, the EU has been accused of exercising too much control over Britain, and thus reducing its ability to make laws for itself. For many voters, this was a step too far.

*There are a number of reasons which explain
why people voted to leave the EU*

4

WHY DID PEOPLE VOTE TO REMAIN?

It is also sensible and fair to include why 48% of British people (on the losing side) voted to remain in the European Union. Many of those who voted to remain wanted stability in the political system, and did not want to take a leap which could have had mixed results.

Reasons for remaining in the EU were quite different as compared to the ones for leaving which I will briefly explain below.

Economy

As they always say: it's the economy stupid! For many people who voted to remain, the economic uncertainty and volatility potentially arising from Brexit was too much to lose. Leaving the European Single Market, with all the trade and important treaties brought by it, was simply a risk which went too far for some. Day after day during the referendum campaign, major businesses and financial institutions reported that leaving the EU would have severe negative consequences for the UK's economy and global standing. The International Monetary Fund (IMF), for example, commented that UK's exit from the bloc would cause 'severe regional and global damage'. Such predictions by credible international organisations meant that many people did not want to take the big leap into the uncertain future. The leave campaigns and their supporters labelled such announcements as fear tactics designed to scare the electorate into voting remain, however for many people these were real concerns that could not be dismissed. On top of that, economic predictions by the government and its financial experts were also pessimistic about an exit which compounded some of the reluctance many people had to vote for Brexit.

Working and being together

Many also voted to remain inside the EU because they thought that it was best placed to deal with the everyday challenges people faced. Political parties such as Labour and the Liberal Democrats pushed forward the argument that problems like climate change, global terrorism and income inequality transcended national borders and could only be solved by working together collectively as the EU does. The European Arrest Warrant, for example, allows the UK to extradite criminals who are wanted in other EU member states and vice versa. Also, in terms of the environment, EU standards are applied collectively across the bloc making sure that air quality does not fall below agreed limits. For these reasons many people felt that a vote to leave reflected a shift towards greater isolationism and less internationalism which could impact on the country's ability to cope with future challenges.

In terms of migration, the leave campaign was often too inflammatory at times when it campaigned on the issue. UKIP, for example, campaigned heavily on the issue with its posters which illustrated the 'threat' posed by open borders (I will talk about this in more detail in Chapter 6). The leave campaign also insisted that Turkey was about to join the EU in the near future, which would lead to an influx of migrants into the UK. This sort of migration-led focus alienated many voters in my opinion, who would have wanted a more nuanced, balanced debate about immigration. Also, many people felt that the free movement of people within the EU was beneficial for them. What we must recognise is that EU migration cuts both ways – we can travel freely anywhere within the bloc, and in return, people can travel freely into the UK from member states. Many people had friends and family inside the EU and many wanted to improve their career or retirement prospects by going to different European countries. In this case, these people saw more advantages than disadvantages with the current migration framework and sought to protect the freedoms they had and could possibly enjoy in the future.

5

WHAT DO THE 'EXPERTS' SAY?

As I said in my introduction, the referendum campaign, was at times, quite expert-dominated and often excluded the voices of ordinary people. However, the view from experts should also not be ignored, as their expertise in their respective fields, provides them with new insights and experiences. If we are to make Brexit a success, we need experts like those mentioned in this book to unite together and use their expertise and contacts to push towards progressive change.

As part of this book, I interviewed individuals from all sides of the British political spectrum who voted to leave or remain in the European Union. They were asked to comment on how they saw Britain's future outside the EU. Many offered their time to talk to me about their views and I value their contributions, however not all views could be published due to word constraints. All factual information is correct at the time of publishing.

Stuart Agnew (UKIP) – Member of the European Parliament (campaigned for Britain to leave the European Union)

Stuart Agnew is a Member of the European Parliament for UKIP, representing the East of England region since 2009. Aside from being a MEP, he is also a Norfolk farmer and is a member of the National Farmers Union. He has also worked in farm management, where he was a Soil and Water Conservation Officer in Rhodesia.

1) Major challenges that the UK faces post-Brexit

The challenge that we face in the long term is to genuinely secure our borders without a huge inconvenience to bona fide travellers. There are many people who would like to visit the UK on a short term basis e.g. for holiday and this should not change. In terms of trade, I don't see establishing trading relations as a challenge. Buyers and sellers lead the way on this, politicians merely interfere.

2) Views on resolving differences between those who voted to remain and leave

Many of those who voted to Remain believed in 'project fear'. As time goes by, these concerns are steadily being nullified. Many also believed that only the EU would support science, Erasmus, Horizon 20/20 etc. The UK supported such things pre-EU, but handed over organisational power after joining. Again, as time goes by, serious problems in the Eurozone will continue to unfold, weakening faith in the EU 'dream' and, of course, the migrant crisis will continue to make headlines and this will assure some of the remain voters. Some who voted to Remain have a vested interest (gravy train syndrome) and they, of course, will remain disaffected to some extent. If some 'Remainers' are so disgusted with having to live in a genuine democracy, then emigrating to an EU country is an alternative.

3) Views on how the UK could preserve and enhance its status as an economic and global powerhouse post-Brexit

We could enhance our global image by re-establishing our links with the former Commonwealth and by benefitting from the fact that we speak the international language. Secondly, we could regain our seat on world bodies such as the World Trade Organization (WTO), where formerly the EU represented us. This will allow the UK to look globally, rather than just regionally.

In terms of the way we speak, we must stop talking ourselves down and realise that we have research institutions here that are the envy of the world. We have educational institutions that are pioneers in their respective fields and that will continue to happen. Moreover, we need to ensure that our foreign aid budget is properly targeted at countries that are genuinely in need. Finally, we must start manufacturing what customers actually want, rather than altering specifications to suit EU bureaucrats.

Afzal Khan (Labour) – Member of the European Parliament (campaigned for Britain to remain in the European Union)

Afzal Khan is a Member of the European Parliament, representing North West England who was elected on a

Labour party platform at the 2014 European Parliament elections. Born in Pakistan, he is also a practicing solicitor and was awarded a CBE for his services as a community cohesion advocate.

1) Thoughts on the UK's future outside the EU

Without a doubt, there is a huge task ahead of us in terms of establishing a new relationship with our European partners. The people who campaigned to leave the EU had no concrete plans of what to do and no idea what sort of relationship Britain should have with our neighbouring countries. The future of our country is quite uncertain, and the government of the time must play a more pro-active role in assuring businesses and other financial institutions that their relationship with EU member countries will not be affected.

2) Major challenges after we leave the EU

The major challenge we face is in regards to the economy of our country. The economy is always the backbone of a country and its society, allowing things like road works, housing and funding of public services to take place. What any government needs to ensure is that we have full access to the single market, allowing our goods full penetration into European markets.

Secondly, the other challenge is to make sure that our security and defence capabilities are not compromised. There are many benefits derived from working together. The fight against terrorism and cybercrime requires us to work together with allies around the world, especially with the EU. Russian aggression and adventurism in Eastern Europe even poses a threat to the UK's national security. Without being in a cooperative body such as the EU, the UK must ensure that intelligence sharing continues with the member states.

3) On resolving issues between communities after the referendum vote

Integration is one of the most pressing needs in 21st century society as we live in a global village where we are increasingly interconnected and interdependent. The challenge after such a bruising referendum campaign, is how we, and governments use public space in an effective way which brings people together. What must also be done is that our public institutions represent the communities that they serve. Politicians and community leaders from all sides must make sure that after this result we positively celebrate our diversity, rather than just tolerate it.

4) Views on the leave campaigns stance on controlling EU migration

The greatest tragedy of the referendum result is that the leave campaign has been lying without any reservation – and their focus on immigration represents this. They do not want to be hold to account anymore which is extremely worrying. The truth about immigration is that it has done great wonders for our country. We are Great Britain only because of our richness and diversity which comes through our multi-cultural society. Some of the concerns people have with immigration, which were exacerbated by the leave campaign, are actually due to inadequate government spending on housing, education and hospitals. What the leave campaigners blindly ignored was the fact that EU migration is a two-way process, which allowed British people to travel to European countries in order to pursue their chosen career paths or for old people to enjoy their retirement. Many of our universities have benefitted from increased revenue through the arrival of EU students which has funded research and development – the leave campaign had completely ignored this. The sole truth is that immigration needs to be managed in a better way, but not by cutting it down to 'tens of thousands' which is what the leave campaign wanted. If immigration is indeed cut down to that amount, then EU and non-EU migrants will probably not be allowed to bring in their relatives and loved ones to visit the UK, and our ability to attract talent from around the world might be affected.

Lord Nazir Ahmed – Member of the House of Lords – (campaigned for Britain to leave the European Union)

Lord Nazir Ahmed started his political career in 1990 as a local Labour Party councillor and he was also the first Asian councillor of Rotherham. He was appointed to the House of Lords as a life peer in 1998 on the recommendation of Tony Blair, the Prime Minister at that time. Aside from his political responsibilities, he is a property developer and helps various humanitarian and charitable causes around the world.

His views on the referendum result

I firmly believe that the UK will be a more outward-looking, prosperous country in the future due to leaving the EU. The EU has imposed several rules and regulations which has stifled our growth and economic development in the past. We will now be able to work and trade more robustly with markets across the world, including major global powerhouses such as China and the United States. Also, we have a huge opportunity awaiting us in the Commonwealth countries – places which we had wilfully neglected due to our membership of the European Union. The future of Britain is looking more positive in my opinion, as we would be able to reach out to places all around the world in search of new opportunities, experiences and ideas. History has shown that Britain is a proud nation, and with determination and hard work everything is within our reach.

Although many xenophobic elements in our country have taken advantage of the fact that we have voted to leave the EU and are pushing forward their racist, Islamophobic agenda, grass root initiatives are urgently needed to bring together communities. Racism has always existed in one form or another. To suggest that it has purely risen due to the referendum result would be unjust. Islamophobic sentiments have been stirred up by racist groups such as Pegida in Germany, and this is filtering into our British society. The government must work together with faith leaders to ensure that no group is allowed to divide our society through hate speech and racial incitement.

Dr Rami Ranger MBE – Businessman – (campaigned for Britain to remain in the European Union)

Raminder Singh Ranger is a British-Indian entrepreneur who is founder of Sun Mark, which is a global marketing and distribution company and Sea, Air & Land Forwarding. He set up his first business with just £2 capital in 1987 from a shed in Hayes. His two companies received the Queen's Award for Enterprise on five occasions: 2009, 2010, 2011, 2012 & 2013 and he was also named the Man of the Year at the GG2 Leadership Awards in London where David Cameron presented the award. Apart from his business activities, Dr Ranger is also involved in philanthropic work through his donations to universities and the Shaheed Nanak Singh Foundation which he set up himself.

1) Main challenges facing the UK post-Brexit

The main challenge facing Britain in the short term is to keep the union with Scotland and Northern Ireland intact, as both of them had voted to remain in the European Union. Secondly, the long challenge will be to disengage from the European Union having been part of it for over 40 years. The disengagement must ensure that there is no animosity between the former trading partners and most of the trade remains unaffected.

2) Resolving the divide between the people who voted to remain and leave

In a democracy, the majority will always prevail. Britain being a civilised nation, the people will accept the verdict of the majority. As prominent government leaders have made clear, Brexit means Brexit and as a result, there is no going back. People must recognise this.

3) Views on how Britain can preserve and enhance its status as an economic and global powerhouse post-Brexit

UK has always been a player on the world stage. It is the 5th largest economy in the world and a member of the United Nations Security Council. Her Majesty the Queen is the Head of the Commonwealth with deep relations with member states going back centuries.

The Commonwealth countries like India, Pakistan, Australia, Canada, New Zealand, South Africa and so on are already doing substantial business with Britain and now the opportunity has come to grow this business even more. Japan and China already have a significant investment in Britain and as a result, their relationship will not be affected. Britain has a special relationship with America and there is no doubt that this relationship will continue. Besides, Britain is a net importer from the European Union and it will be difficult for these countries to upset their own trade with Britain as it will affect them more.

Janice Atkinson (Independent) – Member of the European Parliament (campaigned for Britain to leave the European Union)

Janice Atkinson is an independent Member of the European Parliament, representing the South East region of England. Prior to becoming an MEP, she ran a marketing business and was also a member of the Conservative Party. In the 2010 General Election, she was also the Conservative candidate for the Batley and Spen constituency. After joining UKIP in 2011, Atkinson was selected by the party to become a list candidate for the European Parliament and she was successful in 2014 along with a number of UKIP MEPs. At present, she is now an Independent MEP and a member of the Europe of Nations and Freedom, a political grouping in the European Parliament.

1) Major challenges that the UK faces post-Brexit

The main challenge is getting profitable and sustainable trade deals with the rest of the world. This should not be seen as a negative challenge, but a chance to reach out to the world. Countries such as Pakistan, Australia, New Zealand, US, Canada, China, Mexico and India have all indicated that they are willing to do deals with the UK. The real challenge is how dedicated the government is in exploring these new opportunities. The other challenge is getting the EU to see that having a swift and amicable trade deal is in their best interests and ours.

2) Views on how the UK could preserve and enhance its status as an economic and global powerhouse post-Brexit

All the cards are stacked in our favour. We have the City of London which is a global economic powerhouse in its own right – a number of financial institutions have their headquarters here and will continue to have so. We have the strength of the Commonwealth with the potential for trading with all the countries, including many emerging economies that are part of it. On top of that, countless economic powerhouses are queuing up to do free trade deals with Britain.

In order to enhance and preserve our global status, we should lower corporation tax to 10% to attract further inward investment. As well as this, we should lower taxes and VAT, as we will have total control over VAT. This is something we were not able to do under EU law. Moreover, post Brexit we will be able to set out and enhance our own judicial system and deport criminals and illegal immigrant faster. This will send a clear message to the rest of the world that Britain is a not a soft touch, but a country which has the willpower to carry out tough decisions which are in the national interest.

3) Views on resolving differences between those who voted to remain

The 48% of those who voted to remain have to accept the democratic will of the 52%. Once we have established free trade deals with the rest of the world, then the fears of those who voted remain will die down and become unfounded. Quite a lot of people, many who voted to remain, were worried about travel. This will not change. We are not in Schengen and had reciprocal agreements with countries beforehand. We have around 400,000 French nationals in the UK and countless British people own property and work in France – this will not change. Our politicians must keep reminding people about this. The 48% of those who voted to remain were also worried about funding concerns for industries and our universities. Let me tell them this very clearly. Our universities and sciences will have more money to spend as we are not reliant on UK taxpayers' money that is sent to the EU, siphoned off and then sent back again. Reciprocal arrangements for education will continue. Also, our fishing industry will be able to grow again. It was decimated by 50% under the Common Fisheries Policy. We can now preserve our own stocks of fish and take back control of our waters, currently being plundered by industrial scale fishing. These optimistic messages will go a long way in resolving the divide between those who voted to remain and leave.

Dr Akbar Malik – British Immigration lawyer

Dr Akbar Malik is a well-known British immigration lawyer. He manages his own law firm called Malik Law Chambers, which has offices throughout the UK. Handling a wide range of immigration-related cases, Mr Malik is an advocate of human rights and is passionate about making the British immigration system more fair and transparent. In 2016 he launched a new political party, Immigrants Political Party, which aims to promote the interests and rights of immigrants who reside in the UK.

1) Challenges which the UK faces post-Brexit

The primary challenge Britain faces is in extricating itself from the deep economic, political, legal and social roots it had signed up to. I also believe that it will have a significant impact on the consciousness of British people who were identifying themselves with the idea of being an EU national. However, in the long term Britain will form similar relationships with Commonwealth countries which will allow it to prosper economically. The other challenge post-Brexit is for Britain to adopt a fairer, sustainable immigration system. I think that immigration will open up to other countries – more on a global scale, rather than on a EU level.

2) Resolving the divide between those who voted to leave and remain

There is no real conflict, albeit it seems that there is. Many people who voted to leave the EU did so because they were fed up that the UK was sending too much money to the EU, and they felt that they were not seeing any significant improvement in their own quality of life. The fact that 48% of people voted to remain in the EU brings confidence to other European countries that our country does not hate the EU and that there is a level of mutual tolerance and respect for other Europeans.

3) Views on how the UK can preserve and enhance its status as an economic and global powerhouse when it leaves the EU

The UK does not need to enhance its status as an economic powerhouse when it leaves the UK, as the country already has great credentials globally. I do not worry about this as there are other ties the UK has with other parts of the world and our country is greatly respected world-wide for all kinds of things – this includes our economy, education system and infrastructure. Of course, there is the fear that existing investors may decide to leave the UK and take their companies with them – but that vacuum will easily be filled by other economic superpowers who will invest in this country.

6

EU RESULT AND RACE RELATIONS

The result of the EU referendum, and the campaign in general has opened up a massive fault-line in British politics, which has led to the division of many communities in our society. The binary nature of a referendum means that some sort of division and polarisation within the electorate is inevitable. However, on multiple occasions during the referendum campaign, it seemed as if things were getting out of hand. In order to gain voter approval, both the leave and remain campaigns resorted to bold, ill-thought statements which angered certain sections of the electorate.

How was the referendum campaign conducted?

Following the referendum result, Baroness Sayeeda Warsi, who was the co-Chair of the Conservative Party between 2010 and 2012, commented on how the campaign to leave the EU was quite 'divisive and xenophobic'. To some extent this statement is quite valid. At times, the campaign to leave the EU had seemed to be hijacked by the likes of UKIP and right wing sentiments, who wanted the campaign to be purely focused on immigration. Even moderate leave figures on the right, including Boris Johnson and Michael Gove, sensed that migration was a key issue which could turn voters to their side, and therefore their language on EU migrants was also not suitable at times for a diverse country such as ours.

Although the free movement of people was a genuine issue to campaign on, the way EU migrants were described was certainly not very ethical or sensible. Words like 'swarm', 'overwhelming' and 'burden' were repeatedly thrown around about European migrants on social media and through certain campaign literature which was published, which created a social divide which was similar to what caused numerous race riots in our towns and cities in the past. One clear example was the poster titled 'Breaking Point' which was unveiled by Nigel Farage, and his party UKIP, which depicted a line of Syrian refugees waiting to enter European borders. This poster, which was met with condemnation from all major political leaders, played upon people's concerns regarding immigration and attempted to label anyone foreign, as somewhat dangerous and a burden on British society. Posters created by the unofficial Brexit campaign, Leave.EU, also seemed to draw parallels between the Orlando shootings that killed 49 people in June 2016, with the need to protect the UK from the EU's free movement of people. This sort of scaremongering seeked to create a divide between 'them' and 'us', reminiscent of Edward Said's notion of Orientalism.

Were all leavers old, white and racist?

In the aftermath of the referendum result, there have been many social media posts which have smeared those who voted to leave as xenophobic and inward looking 'little Englanders'. As Paul Lewis, a freelance financial journalist and broadcaster on BBC television and radio put it: 'Of course not all leavers are racist. That would be a terrible thought. But all racists now think 52% of the population agree with them'. It is true that right wing groups and organisations such as UKIP, Britain First and BNP campaigned for Britain to leave the EU, however that does not mean that every person who voted to leave resembles the characteristics of these groups.

For example, in the London borough of Wandsworth where I live, I came across many people from the Asian community which I belong to who voted to leave the European Union. Contrary to stereotypes, these 'leavers' were not xenophobes or narrow minded, but believed in a multicultural society and voted to leave because they wanted a fairer immigration system in which both EU and non-EU migrants are given the same opportunities when it comes down to working and living in the UK. Many places which have a high Black, Asian and minority ethnic (BAME) population such as Bradford voted to leave – 54.2% voted to leave the EU in Bradford. Moreover, Muslims for Britain was a campaign set up by

Muslim businessmen who campaigned around the country for Britain's exit from the EU and their message was not based upon nationalism or a narrow minded agenda, but one in which they wanted Britain to embrace the Commonwealth countries which have contributed immensely to the social fabric of our country.

Dismissing the referendum result as a win for xenophobes and inward-looking people, will make things even worse. We need to be bringing people together rather than isolating them.

Racial tensions in the aftermath of the result

Initial figures by the National Police Chief's Council suggested a 57% increase in reported racial incidents following the vote to leave the EU. Reports included racist graffiti on entrances of Polish community centres and hate posts online telling people to 'go back home'. Whether this is due to the referendum result, or whether people are more willing to report incidents is still quite uncertain. But the fact is that tensions in communities are becoming more apparent than ever. The divide between the 51% who voted to leave and the 48% who voted to remain, in my opinion, has been turned into a divide between the 'narrow minded xenophobes' vs 'the internationalist liberals'. Many of our media outlets and politicians are to blame for this misrepresentation.

In the aftermath of the referendum result, many of my very close friends who have come to the UK from various European countries, are deeply distressed about the spike in racial attacks targeted at them. Speaking to many European migrants on the street, it is clear that they feel as if the referendum result is a vote against their presence in the UK and a vote against their livelihoods. To show this to the readers, here are the views of two Eastern European migrants who live in London and who I have spoken to on the streets of London (names have been changed to protect the privacy of individuals):

Julia (22, from Poland): 'Everything after the result seems so different. I was proud to be a European, travelling around the continent, meeting different people from various walks of life. All that has changed now. Although many people have been friendly and supportive since I came to London in 2010, I feel as if leaving the European Union has really divided livelihoods and lives, especially mine. The Polish centre near to where I live has received a lot of hate mail which has really frightened the local Polish community. We are hard-working individuals who really want to contribute towards British society. The things that Nigel Farage has said about people from Eastern Europe has really left a mark on how some people view us, and I think that will never change'.

Adam (36, from Bulgaria): 'The referendum result completely shocked me. I never thought that the British people would vote to leave. I work hard, pay my taxes and live a normal life to contribute towards this country and support my wife and kids who are in Bulgaria. My family are really concerned about me but I have assured them that everything will be fine. Walking home from work after a night- shift a couple of days after the referendum, I was talking to my parents on the phone who are in Bulgaria. A couple of people in the mid-twenties starting shouting at me, telling me 'that my time is up' and that I should 'go back to where I came from'. This really brought my morale down. I just don't feel wanted anymore. Many people have been kind to me, ever since I arrived in the UK. But events like these certainly leave a bad taste'.

Secondly, this referendum result does not just represent a vote for more sovereignty back to Westminister, it represents the way Brits see their diverse and multicultural society. The 2016 Global Attitudes Survey, conducted by the PEW Research Center, reports that 31% of people surveyed in the UK suggested that diversity made the country a worse place to live, whereas 34% suggested it didn't make any difference. I think the vote to leave represents this. Some of the people who voted to leave did so in fear that their communities were being overwhelmed by foreign people. And the sad fact is that the media, and many of our politicians have not celebrated the positives derived from being a multicultural, multi-ethnic society. Issues regarding multiculturalism and assimilation are coming to the forefront more prominently after the referendum result which is fuelling more racialized tension in our society. There has been too much talk in regards to stressing the importance of integration, and less celebration of what diversity entails and enables our nation to do. A balance must be struck between celebrating diversity and encouraging integration.

Well, then how can we reduce the racial tensions in the aftermath of the vote? The answer, as with everything, is quite complex and ambiguous. Primarily, it must be the job of any current and future government to bring together faith groups of all sects and denominations alongside prominent leave campaigners, to denounce any form of xenophobia, particularly one which has emerged out of this referendum result. Positive reporting about Britain's future outside the European Union by the media may also ease racial tensions, as many racialized attacks may have been caused due to frustration. This may be as a result of the negative and pessimistic attitude adopted by the people after the referendum who wanted to remain in the EU. More importantly, most of this racial tension exists on online platforms such as social media where people are free to share what they like and comment on a wide range of issues. Internet providers and social media companies must work together to suffocate any xenophobia which exists, by taking action against any form of abuse or use of racial slurs. There is a very fine line between free speech and offensive language, and some social media posts which I have seen after the referendum campaign have crossed this barrier.

Reducing tensions perpetuated through the referendum campaign and result will take a long time to subside. The solutions I have mentioned in the paragraph above all seem to be viable and productive, but their implementation is the key thing. Parliament, for once, must focus upon legislating and implementing more robust anti-discrimination and anti-racism laws which prosecute organisations and people who seek to divide society through abuse and unacceptable rhetoric. Regardless of political affiliation and ideology, all parties must work together and understand that any form of hatred and xenophobia is detrimental to the foundation of our diverse, multicultural society. The other issue concerns the wellbeing of EU citizens who are currently residing in Britain and contribute positively towards the betterment of the country. I suggest that Parliament should carry out detailed consultations with EU citizens who are living in Britain by asking them what sort of abuse, if any, they are facing. These consultations must also ask these people the different places in which racist abuse is taking place. This will help the government and police authorities to allocate resources to the worst hit areas. Such consultations must also reach out to all ethnic minority communities, as they are also affected by the menace of racism.

7

REFERENDUM 2.0?

Could there ever be another referendum on our membership of the European Union? Will we join it again?

There has been a lot of speculation regarding the possibility of another referendum on our membership of the European Union. Gossip in the social media circle says that even though the country has voted to leave, we will eventually join the political bloc in the future. Such a scenario in my opinion is possible.

Referendums should be a once in a lifetime opportunity. Holding another referendum could set a very negative precedent in the future for electoral politics. Re-runs after re-run. Voter fatigue and apathy is already on the rise, as election turnout results show and a re-run of this referendum could de-moralise many voters who turned out for the first time to vote to leave or remain. A turnout of 72.2%, the highest turnout in a UK-wide vote since the 1992 general elections is a strong enough mandate which should be respected. I also think that there is no political appetite for another referendum. After the vote to leave, the government and related institutions are already engaged in detailed negotiations about the future economic and political future of the UK and would not want to waste their time on another referendum campaign which could be costly and highly time consuming.

Although referendum results are not legally binding, the will of the 51.9% must be respected. People calling for the vote to be ignored or for a re-run, are not liberals or internationalists. These are anti-democratic people and those who treat voter concerns with disdain – the same sort of behaviour which has alienated large chunks of the electorate.

Another key contentious issue is whether we should join the European Union again in the future if conditions are to our liking. Such a scenario is entirely plausible in my opinion. For that to happen, the EU must change significantly to suit Britain's needs, in terms of tightening free movement of people and returning more powers to national parliaments. Some may call it wishful thinking, but I would disagree. The wave of Euroscepticism in many of the existing member states, including influential members such as Germany and Spain could force the EU to accommodate difference and alter the rules in order to prevent the bloc from disintegration and break up. In such a scenario, it might be in Britain's best interest to contemplate joining back again. However, this must take place by consulting with the electorate first who should hold ultimate power. Immigration and sovereignty were two of the main issues which dominated the referendum campaign in my opinion, and if the EU could resolve those then anything is possible. EU federalists and leaders are slowly recognising that 'business as usual' is not going to be beneficial and soon they will be forced to show flexibility.

8

FRAGMENTED POLITICS

A lot has been spoken about the long term future of Britain's economy, migration policy and society due to a vote to leave the European Union. The political future of the country, however, is the most important factor that must be considered. A vote to leave has significant ramifications for the political future of the four main parties in British politics: Conservatives, Labour, Liberal Democrats and UKIP.

Conservatives

Historically, the Conservative Party has been split down the middle on the issue of the European Union. Even during the referendum campaign, this was very clear. Although the official position of the government was to stay in the EU, around 138 Tory MPs voted to leave, compared to 185 who were remainers (approximate figures). Michael

Gove, Chris Grayling and Priti Patel were also a number of prominent Cabinet members who defied the government and campaigned strongly to leave. At one point this deep division seemed to put the future of the party in jeopardy, including the risk of political defections or resignations.

Despite these divisions, the long term future of the party looks secure and positive. A vote to leave has satisfied the long-term Eurosceptic members of the party, both inside Parliament and amongst the grassroots membership. Those who aligned with an anti-EU stance have achieved their long-term held ambition – this will limit any other opposition in the party for the foreseeable future and a move towards UKIP, who have achieved their raison d'être. The main problem, however, lies in bringing together those in the party who voted to remain. Many of those who voted to remain within the party would understandably be feeling let down by the result. These individuals might seek to find an alternative, more moderate political home, possibly the Liberal Democrats which is the only party fully committed to the European cause in my opinion. If pro-EU forces, such as Labour, the Green Party, Liberal Democrats, SNP and Plaid Cymru join up in the future to push for a British re-entry into the EU then the Conservative party's Europhile faction might reconsider their allegiance. This wholly depends on the future direction of the Conservative Party and how it seeks to unite and accommodate opposing views in terms of Europe.

Labour

Traditionally a party which appeals to the working class masses of the country, Labour's political future remains quite uncertain after the EU referendum. Despite being a pro-EU party and campaigning strongly to remain in the bloc, many Labour voters turned towards the Brexit option. In the Labour heartlands of North-east, for example, 11 out of the 12 authorities voted to leave the EU (778,103 voted to leave). Sunderland, Gateshead, Hartlepool, Darlington – and the list carries on. And the striking thing is that these are the areas which have returned Labour MPs for decades. Many voters in Labour areas such as Hartlepool felt that the free movement of people was simply not working in their favour, leading to a lower quality of life than already exists.

Such a result throws up all sorts of questions for the Labour Party. How should it reach out to those disaffected voters in the North and other parts of the UK who voted to leave? Should it change its overall message? Should it move more towards the centre of the political spectrum? These are questions which will probably be persisting in the minds of many Labour voters and hard-working activists. The real fear is that disaffected Labour voters who voted to leave the EU may try finding an alternative political home – in this case it might be UKIP. UKIP already has a substantial presence in the North of England where it has soaked up support from the old, white working class population and it will continue to push forward in those areas in order to build a more robust electoral vote for future elections. This complicates Labour's future even more. The party must start discussing issues such as immigration more loudly, and not just dismiss them as it has been accused of doing. More importantly, the sad reality is that Labour has often lurched to different sides of the political spectrum under different leaders – to the right under Tony Blair, and to the left under Jeremy Corbyn. There is a real appetite in British politics for a moderate, centre leaning party which reaches out to all sections of the electorate. The Liberal Democrats, sadly, have so far failed to do this. Labour needs to move towards the centre of British politics if it is to become a 'one nation party', reaching across to voters throughout the four nations of the United Kingdom.

Liberal Democrats

Suffering somewhat of an electoral oblivion in the 2015 General Election, the Liberal Democrats have already known that they must change their overall message and approach. I believe that this strongly pro-EU party has a more positive future in the long term as it targets the 48% who voted to remain. During the referendum campaign, the nature of political discourse shifted from the left to the right of British politics and vice versa very quickly which created a political vacuum for a moderate, progressive voice. The message that it is trying to highlight of a socially progressive, internationalist European identity would interest a large section of the electorate who feel that the decision to leave the EU has negative ramifications for them and their society. Being the only centre-left party in British politics in my opinion, it has a good chance of attracting support from Tories who voted to remain, and Labour voters who are disaffected by the state of the two main parties.

UKIP

UKIP's raison d'être was leaving the EU. Since its formation in 1993, the party has campaigned exclusively on an anti-EU platform which allowed it to gain seats in the European Parliament. Led by Nigel Farage, its leader, that task has now been accomplished. What future does UKIP have now?

UKIP's future, as many party members and commentators argue lies in soaking up disaffected Labour voters in the North of England who view their party as being too metropolitan and London centred. White, working class and middle aged/ elderly voters are the demographic that UKIP will heavily focus on in the future in order to get a stronger foothold into first-past-the-post politics. But as the issue of Britain's membership of the EU has been settled through the referendum result, many voters are thinking that the party is a spent force because it can no longer campaign on European related issues which it was seen as being more competent at. This is where the party will fundamentally change its position. The party will now try to focus on issues of healthcare (i.e. the NHS), the economy and parliamentary reform – all issues which it previously neglected to some extent. As the issue of free movement of people into the UK from the EU dies down as a result of the EU referendum, my fear is that UKIP might start targeting the numbers of people coming from outside the EU in order to shore up its immigrant sceptic base. There is a real vacuum in British politics for a party which speaks its mind out and rejects political correctness, and I think UKIP can fill this role in the long term.

Future direction of all these parties

From what I have spoken about above, it is very clear that British politics will never stay the same again. This referendum result could be considered a wake-up call for all the main Westminister parties, a result which will leave a long term footprint on the future of our political system. A fragmented form of politics is emerging, where party policies and pledges may change and where intraparty differences will become more apart. What is clear is that stability in the political system is required. Although voters want radical and swift change in how politics is done, political parties across the board must not turn to populism which is already a danger affecting some European countries.

After this referendum, all political parties must come out of the 'Westminister bubble' and realise that voter concerns need to be addressed more effectively. For that, parties need to reflect the British population. This means more state school educated MPs, more BME politicians and governmental officials who have had experience of working outside of politics. I think this fundamental re-think will happen in the backrooms of politics where political parties will try and think of how they can reach out to all sections of the electorate. More importantly, this referendum has been a win for direct democracy. The Scottish independence referendum in 2014 and the EU vote all saw record high voter turnout on issues which were highly important for the future of the country. Political parties in the future will try and mimic this form of direct democracy in their own internal politics. Don't be surprised if parties start consulting their registered members to vote on proposed policy and future manifesto pledges. Beppe Grillo's Five Star Movement in Italy has been quite successful and it has incorporated a model of direct democracy policy making in its organisation. Many political parties in Britain can learn from it. Parties from across the political spectrum are starting to realise that voters feel more content with the political system when they are engaged more directly with decision making.

Although there are some negative effects from leaving the European Union, one positive is that our political parties will have more things to debate on. As more legislative powers and policy areas return from Brussels to Westminister, all political parties will have more responsibility. Policy areas such as immigration, trade, foreign affairs and agricultural policy will be debated more thoroughly in Parliament, giving political parties a greater opportunity to show their skills and target their core voters.

9

UNCERTAIN FUTURE AHEAD

'It is not in the stars to hold our destiny but in ourselves' (William Shakespeare).

Whether we like it or not, our future, even after the referendum result is inextricably connected to the future of the European Union. We are geographically located in Europe, our major trading partners are our European allies and in terms of security and defence arrangement, we need to work closely with our European partners. Signs from the rest of Europe are not looking very positive. According to a study conducted by the PEW Research Centre in 2016, Euroscepticism is on the rise all across Europe. In France, for example, 61% view the European Union unfavourably, and in Greece the figure is as high as 71%. This deep disconnect with the European project has fuelled the rise of Eurosceptic far right-wing, populist parties across Europe. National Front, led by Marine

Le Pen in France, and the Geert Wilders' Party for Freedom in Netherlands are becoming more potent forces in their own domestic politics and are increasingly garnering the support of the electorate due to their tough stance on immigration and the associated migrant crisis. I am not suggesting that Euroscepticism is necessarily a bad thing, but combined with far-right xenophobia and rampant nationalism, this potion could potentially seep from Europe into British politics more fervently.

<u>Why we should listen to the 48%</u>

Although a majority of 51% voted to leave the EU, and we should respect the decision, 48% voted differently. Dismissing the anxieties and concerns of the 48% would be a massive mistake for our country, creating even more divisions in our society than already exist. Moving on from the childish, political infighting which was seen during the referendum campaign, representatives from the leave and remain campaigns must come together and focus on finding a middle-of-the road consensus which creates a relationship with our European allies that appeases both sides. It will be difficult, no doubt, but there is far more which unites us than divides us.

What we must also understand is that not all of the 48% who voted to remain were Europhiles. Many of them were also Eurosceptics but did not want to take a risk which could lead to economic uncertainty and risk for them and their families.

Future governments must strongly ensure that economic policy works in favour of ordinary households who are the first to be hit when there is an economic shock or slump. People who voted to remain must be encouraged to think more positively, as a positive mind-set by the whole nation will make our divorce with the EU more profitable in the long term.

An overwhelming number of young people voted to remain in the EU, and understandably they will be quite distraught and let down by the result. Young people are our future, and they have an important stake in the running of our nation. For decades, politicians have failed to connect with young people in understanding their concerns and anxieties. Working together with the younger generation is required more than ever following the referendum result. The stereotyping of young people as politically disengaged, lazy and not aspirational needs to be put to rest and politicians should work closely with young people to understand what particular sections of UK's EU membership they cherished and wanted to preserve. Post-Brexit policy should not hamper the educational opportunities available to young people. An agreement with our EU partners must be arranged which allows young people to study around Europe without stringent restrictions.

Britain's status as a global nation

Voting to leave the European Union was a monumental change in British political history, and I presume will lead to economic uncertainty for many years to come. This uncertainty does not need to be seen in a negative way, but could also serve as more of an incentive for Britain to be more optimistic and outward looking. By leaving the EU, more emphasis is now being placed on Britain's trading relationship with the rest of the world. I would argue that we are in the best placed position to project our global status, even by leaving the EU. Many emerging markets such as China and India are undergoing a seismic shift. They are moving away from their reliance on cheap exports towards increased domestic consumption. As the middle class population in these countries increases, so will demand for financial services as well as creative content such as films and video games. Being the knowledge-based economy Britain is, we as a country will be best served in selling our services to these countries.

Too often our trade agreements and relations have been made by bureaucrats and politicians. Although these people are quite competent at what they do, many lack financial or real life job experience outside of politics. A Britain outside the EU must have businessmen and businesswomen at the forefront of the trade negotiation table. We need our business community to build stronger links with the government so that they can help Britain establish trade deals with countries around the world in a more effective way. Businesses have the relevant skills, contacts and values to reach out to different sorts of people and this is a skill needed more than ever in a post-Brexit Britain.

Also, as the referendum result has indicated, the current scale of immigration to the UK is completely unsustainable and not conducive in promoting a diverse, multi-cultural and cohesive society. Arbitrary figures on the numbers of people that should be allowed to come into Britain, such as the 'tens of thousands' figure proposed by David Cameron, is not viable and realistic. But what I do know is that a Britain outside the EU will be able to bring in talent from all around the world, regardless of race, gender and nationality. Under EU rules, people coming from the EU are allowed free movement to any of the member states, whereas non-EU migrants face visa restrictions through a points based system. A global Britain, outside the EU, will be able to apply fairness in its immigration system, allowing talent from Europe, the Commonwealth and the rest of the world to contribute to our country. Allowing an Egyptian nurse, Syrian doctor, Polish accountant and an Indian computer scientist to contribute to British services will become even more possible when we are more outward looking outside the EU. Being an immigrant myself, I hope that Britain adopts a migration policy which is fit for the 21st century, one which realises that difference and diversity triumphs.

The onus is now on Parliament

Before and during the referendum campaign there was a lot of talk about the proportion of UK law that was made by the EU. As usual, different figures from the opposing sides were thrown around, confusing the electorate even more – Nigel Farage suggested it was 75%, whilst Nick Clegg said it was 7% in a 2014 LBC debate. The House of Commons Library itself conceded that there is no real accurate way to make the calculation of what percentage of laws are made where.

Regardless of the figure, now that Britain has voted to leave the EU, Parliament will need to play more a pro-active role in legislating for the British people. As more powers are returned from Brussels to Westminister, Parliament must legislate more on the issues which concern ordinary, hard-working people. This will require MPs to be more conscious of the views of their constituents who they represent. Greater power entails more responsibility, and Parliament must not follow the top-down notion which the EU has followed. Instead, it must give more power to the lower levels of policy making, including councils and many of the devolved assemblies that exist. This will ensure that every person and organisation that forms part of our society is content.

Parliament needs to play a more pro-active role in British politics

Why the European Union must change quickly

If there is one thing that this referendum result has taught us, it would be that the European Union has not worked in everyone's interest. Many ordinary people across Europe feel that the political project is quite far away from them, an entity which is not listening to their everyday concerns and becoming increasingly centralised. A testament to this is the statement by the Czech Prime Minister, Bohuslav Sobotka, who, after the referendum, said: 'We need to change the overall functioning of the EU and I think it is needed to change the functioning of the European Commission'. The European federalists in Brussels and Strasbourg need to listen to the demands of many of the member states for more powers to be brought back to national parliaments and thus a more de-centralised EU is urgently required. If the EU is left to function on a 'business as usual' approach, then many other countries will adopt the route that Britain has taken. What the EU has failed to recognise is that every country is economically, politically, socially and demographically different. A catch-all, standardised policy system which the EU operates is not suitable for every country, and the Greece financial crisis is a fine example.

In the face of major challenges such as the migrant crisis, rising terrorism attacks and border security, the EU has failed to provide effective leadership and governance. The EU was formed to act as a consensus building bloc in which member states debated and understood each other's approach to governance and diplomacy. The opposite has happened. Over the last few years, the EU has increasingly acted as a top-down organisation where the Council of Ministers, the overarching executive body, makes all the laws that would govern the member states. Members of the European Parliament have no legal authority to initiate legislation - their sole purpose is to vote on legislation which comes from above. Surely this must change. Surely this is not how a democracy should function. This democratic deficit is one which the European Union needs to address as soon as possible, or otherwise other countries will follow Britain's way.

The EU must start debating and formulating plans on things that matter the most. I have been following developments in the European Parliament very closely for the last few years and have gained a better insight into how policy is debated and agreed up. A lot of the time, things such as roaming call charges, agricultural produce sizes and driving regulations are discussed quite frequently in Brussels. I am not saying that these issues are insignificant, however more attention should be given to other issues. Reducing income equality, increasing international cooperation and improving regional economies. These are the key points which the EU Parliament needs to discuss in more depth and with more conviction in my opinion. Re-adjusting its priorities to focus on more fundamental issues will enable the EU to become a beacon for progressive change for its member states.

*The European Union must start focusing
on the issues which really matter*

The EU must also change, as Euroscepticism is slowly increasing in many member states. A couple of years ago Eurosceptics were often seen as outsiders and a political embarrassment in the EU Parliament and related institutions. The tables have changed now. In fact, pro-EU countries are proving harder to find as time goes by. From regional to national politics, Eurosceptics are making inroads throughout Europe, threatening the existence of the political bloc. It is clear that an ever closer union is not a possibility anymore, as many ordinary people do not want it. Britain's decision to leave the European Union has given hope to many Eurosceptic factions across the member states, who had assumed that leaving the political bloc was never possible. My prediction is that Britain will not be the odd one out – other countries will follow suit. After Brexit, we could possibly see Grexit (Greece), Nexit (Netherlands) or Frexit (France).

Here are a few countries where anti-EU sentiment has been emerging over time:

1) *France:*

Euroscepticism in France is a lot different to the one found in the UK. British Euroscepticism has generally been of a 'hard' nature where the foundations of the EU have been challenged and discredited by certain factions. French Euroscepticism can be described as being 'soft' because only certain aspects of EU membership are critiqued. The most interesting development in France is the rise of the National Front, a far-right, anti EU party which has gained ground in French politics. National Front has merged its socially conservative agenda with left wing economic policies to attract disaffected voters across the country. The party has been particularly vocal against the EU where it has raised opposition against the Euro and the free movement of people.

2) *Germany:*

One would expect Germany to be quite pro-EU, as it has dominated the workings of the bloc for a long time. To a large extent this is true, but cracks are emerging in this relationship. Through my research, I have found that many Germans have become disillusioned with the political project as they fear that they might have to send more of their money to help bailout struggling Eurozone members in order to save the currency union. Apart from that, the migrant crisis, in which the country has taken in over a 1 million refugees has created resentment. The failure of the EU to offer a sustainable solution to the migrant crisis has increased anger within many people. Coupled with this, Germany has its own equivalent of the National Front. The right-wing party, Alternative for Germany (AfD), has steadily become a prominent political force in Germany – it performed quite strongly in the 2016 state elections where it came 2nd in a number of regions. The party also opposes further European integration. Although the possibility of a Germany exit from the EU is not foreseeable, resentment is slowly bubbling up which might create disputes in the long term.

3) *Netherlands:*

Netherlands has historically been a pro-EU country. It was one of the founding member of the European Coal and Steel Community which emerged in 1952. However, even then, anti-EU sentiment is rising. Led by Geert Wilders, the Party for Freedom has performed well in regional elections and is adopting a hard-line stance on the EU which it believes has been detrimental for the continent. The biggest divide was evident in the 2016 referendum, when 61% of Dutch voters rejected an EU treaty on closer ties with Ukraine. This referendum results gives an early indicator as to what the future direction of EU – Netherlands relationship will be.

Why isolationism will not work

Globalisation, whether for the good or bad, is a defining character of our time. The fluid movement of goods, ideas and people represents a world which is highly interconnected and interdependent, spread out like a web of connections which are very hard to untangle from. The UK has always been proud of its internationalist image, whether in terms of providing humanitarian aid or forging stronger relationships with allies around the world – and it must stay this way.

Some of the people who pushed through the agenda to leave the European Union (a very small minority I want to stress) want Britain to revert back to the past, a past in which arrogance, dominance and egoism characterised much of our nations actions. We must not let this happen. Leaving the EU is a historical step, one in which we are looking out at the world in terms of trade and strategic co-operation. With that comes the need for flexibility and restraint. When it comes to negotiating and dealing with international partners, things might not always go our way and people from around the world may disagree with how we approach different problems. This is where the UK must become more accommodating by coping with differences and forging agreements based on mutual respect. The British Empire disintegrated a long time ago and some people must understand that.

<u>Cross cultural dialogue</u>

As I mentioned earlier in the book, many European people consider this referendum result as a vote against themselves. We must not let them feel this way. We are living in an era where we need to share ideas and this should not stop as a result of our withdrawal from the European Union. Europe has a rich history of cultural heritage, ranging from art, literature, cuisine and philosophy. I strongly believe that our cultural industries must perform a reconciliation role in the future with our European partners. And they are perfectly capable of this. Organising more exhibitions, cross-cultural projects and initiatives will facilitate a relationship which can go beyond national boundaries. Although many voters rejected the notion of freedom of movement, the free movement of talent and enterprise must continue to take place between all nations of Europe.

The future of research and education

Understandably, many of our universities and educational institutions are worried about the effects of Britain's withdrawal from the European Union. Many have also published their own statements in regards to how they see the future of research and higher education and are concerned that funding is under threat from leaving the EU. I think Britain's educational sector can have a bright future outside of the European Union. Primarily, some of the money which the UK contributes to the EU budget can be spent on funding research in British educational institutions. Exiting the EU does not mean we are isolated in terms of educational partnerships and collaboration. The UK will still remain part of organisations such as the G8 Research Council and the European Space Agency, both of which are not related to the EU.

Leaving the European Union sets Britain on a more global path. Like many other educational institutions around the world, including many in America and parts of Asia, British universities will be able to recruit and attract talent from around the world without any bias towards students from any particular part of the world. This also applies to recruiting staff who work in our educational institution. At present, students who come from the European Union are charged the same fees as UK students, whilst students coming from outside of the EU are charged higher fees. Is this fair? A post-Brexit will be able to treat EU and non-EU students who wish to study in Britain equally, by setting fees that allow talent to come from around the world. People from across the political spectrum must recognise that talent, expertise and innovation does not depend on being part of ideologically charged institutions like the EU, but is dependent upon on having the passion to achieve success.

Desire for change

This referendum result showed a desire for change. People turned out to vote, many for the first time, to reject the status quo which had been at the helm of policy and decision making. Interviewing many leave voters as part of this book, it was clear that people were very passionate about changing the way their country was run. As a person who was very sceptical about a vote to leave the EU at first, I believe that politics as usual must change. The way our politics has been running for decades – uninspiring, ignorant of voter needs and placid – must change because voters want this. Let's inject some life into our politics. Parliament must include more young people and a taskforce of politicians who reach out to people from all communities, politically engaged or not, to assure them that the political class is listening to their everyday needs and aspirations.

Whether you were a leave or remain voter, it's time for Britain to be more positive and more entrepreneurial than ever before. Unity is required, and that can only be achieved when people from all sides of the political spectrum come together under one common aim – to make Britain a more successful nation. The EU referendum has opened up a massive crack which threatens to divide us. We must not let this happen. For once, we must leave behind our grudges and personal feuds to work for progressive change. Politics will continue to swing between the left and right depending on the issue of the time, but the only way forward in my opinion is to occupy the sensible, middle ground of political opinion.

The vision for Britain outside the EU can be bright, but we must all work together to make it happen. The ball is in our court.

We must find our own path outside the EU

MORE INFORMATION ABOUT THE EU REFERENDUM

If you would like to find out more about the EU referendum and some of the research done about it, here are some links to explore:

- **www.migrationwatch.uk.org**

  MigrationWatch UK is an independent, immigration and asylum research think-tank which publishes many reports in regards to migration policy.

- **http://www.parliament.uk/eu-referendum**

  Parliament's official website which provides impartial analysis of the UK referendum result. Also includes a reading list which references key journals, books and press articles related to the EU.

- **http://www.electoralcommission. org.uk/find-information-by-subject/ elections-and-referendums/**

past-elections-and-referendums/eu-referendum/ electorate-and-count-information

Includes official, detailed results of the EU referendum, including the breakdown by each local area. Results are also available for download.

- **https://fullfact.org/europe**

The UK's independent fact checking organisation which questions many of claims made in public and political discourse. Includes many questions in regards to the UK's withdrawal from the European Union.

- **http://www.civitas.org.uk/research/europe/**

An independent think tank which aims to deepen public understanding of institutional structures. Includes many published reports which are can be downloaded or bought as books.

- http://www.migrationobservatory.ox.ac.uk/
  projects/brexit

  University of Oxford's migration project which
  provides analysis of immigration and migration
  related topics which particularly affect the
  UK. Includes visualisations, commentaries,
  reports and maps/charts which relate to the
  referendum.

- http://www.bbc.co.uk/news/politics/
  eu_referendum/results

  BBC's interactive section dedicated to the EU
  referendum. There are many digital maps and charts
  available which give a breakdown of the result by each
  local authority.

- http://www.pewresearch.org/

  A non-partisan, American think tank which
  is based in Washington D.C. Includes many
  reports which are published about the EU and
  include in-depth surveys.

- http://ukandeu.ac.uk/

  Funded by the Economic and Social Research Council (ESRC), the website aims to analyse the changing relationship between the UK and the European Union. Includes opinions from policy makers, educational institutions and experts from various academic fields.

- https://yougov.co.uk/news/categories/europe/

  Includes a range of opinion polls which analyse updates happening in regards to the European Union.

- https://next.ft.com/eu-referendum

  The Financial Times section dedicated to Britain's withdrawal from the European Union. Includes commentary from its team of reporters and journalists. Some content is free to view, whereas some requires subscription to FT.

- **http://news.cbi.org.uk/business-issues/ uk-and-the-european-union/**

  The official website of the Confederation of British Industry. Includes business views about Britain's economic future outside the EU.

- **https://www.brexitthemovie.com/**

  A crowdfunded feature-length documentary, directed by Martin Durkin which talks about the reasons why people should vote to leave the European Union. It was produced and made available for viewing during the referendum campaign.

EU/BREXIT GLOSSARY

- **Accession:** in EU terminology it refers to the process through which a country becomes a member of the European Union.

- **Article 50:** an 'exit clause' which details the procedure to leave the EU formally – it has never actually been used before.

- **Brexit:** term referred to Britain's exit from the European Union which happened through a referendum on the 23rd of July, 2016.

- **Common Agricultural Policy (CAP):** direct payments that are given to farmers in EU countries.

- **Council of the European Union (often called the Council of Ministers):** the EU's main decision-making body which represents the national governments of the member states.

- **Democratic deficit:** a term used to describe organisations that are not transparent and democratic in their practices.

- **Directive:** legislation passed by the EU that sets a certain goal for member states to achieve. It is then up to the individual member state to decide how it reaches that goal.

- **ECB (European Central Bank):** the central bank for the Euro area which has responsibility for European monetary policy.

- **Enlargement:** a phase through which the EU includes more countries and becomes a bigger bloc. There have been a number of phases, however the biggest one occurred in 2004 when 10 countries joined.

- **European Parliament:** the directly elected body in the European Parliament. Members of the European Parliament (MEPs) are elected to this body every 5 years.

- **Europhile:** someone who is supportive of EU membership and Europe.

- **Eurosceptic:** someone who is not supportive of EU membership and it's growing influence on the nation state.

- **Eurozone:** EU countries which have adopted the Euro as their common currency – there are 19 countries which have done so.

- **Lisbon Treaty:** an agreement which formed the constitutional basis of the EU.

- **Maastricht Treaty:** a treaty signed on 7 February 1992 by the members of the Economic Community. It set down the foundations for the European Union and the Euro.

- **Multiculturalism:** the view that different cultures must co-exist and be accepted within a single jurisdiction e.g. a country.

- **Pooled sovereignty:** the sharing of decision making powers in systems of international policy making.

- **Regulation:** EU legislation which is enforceable on all member states at once – it is different to a directive.

- **Schengen:** an agreement that has allowed certain EU member countries to remove their border checks to allow the easy movement of people from country to country without passport checks. The UK is not part of it.

- **Single Market:** also known as the internal market, it refers to the tariff free movement of goods and services.

- **Sovereignty:** the ability and authority of a state to govern itself. Eurosceptics argue that the EU has reduced the sovereignty of individual member states.

- **Working Time Directive:** EU legislation which sets limits on working hours.

- **Xenophobia:** hatred for people who are foreign. It is often used alongside the word 'racism'.

ABOUT THE AUTHOR

Atta Ul Haq lives in Tooting, London and is the Chief Editor for the Daily UK Times, one of the largest daily newspaper for the UK based Asian community. He regularly writes articles about current affairs in other newspapers and online publications. Apart from journalism, he is also actively engaged in community activism and has received over 100 awards, including many from government departments for the work that he has done. In his free time he enjoys writing poetry and has published a book titled 'Saada e Haq' which includes many of his poetic work.

NOTES

NOTES

NOTES

NOTES

www.ingramcontent.com/pod-product-compliance
Lightning Source LLC
Chambersburg PA
CBHW050409290526
45786CB00003B/1184